QED Everybody Feels...

Sad

Jane Bingham

QED Publishing

QED

A Catalogue record for this book is available
from the British Library.

ISBN 1 84538 389 3

Written by Jane Bingham
Illustrations Helen Turner
Designed by Alix Wood
Editor Clare Weaver

Publisher Steve Evans
Editorial Director Jean Coppendale
Art Director Zeta Davies

Printed and bound in China

Contents

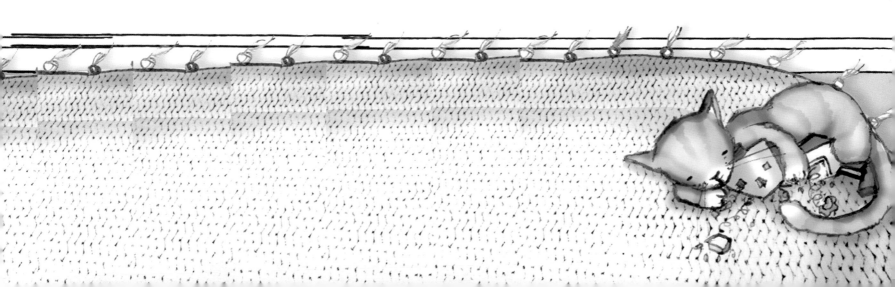

Feeling sad

People have lots of different **feelings**.

They can feel happy.

They can also feel sad.

HAPPY BIRTHDAY

How do you think Sam feels now?

Everyone feels sad sometimes.
When was the last time
you felt sad?

5

How does it feel?

If you are sad, you may feel like crying.

You may want a hug from someone special.

You may also want to spend some time on your own.

Whatever you want to do, it's all right.

Nobody likes feeling sad.

But sadness doesn't last **forever.**

Soon, you will feel happy again.

What makes you sad?

All sorts of things make people feel sad.

Here's what happened to Omar and Amy.

Omar's story

My name is Omar. When I first went to school, some boys were **mean** to me.

They **teased** me and called me names.

At playtime, they didn't let me *join* in their games.

I felt very sad and **lonely**.

11

Then, one day, a boy called Zack **made friends** with me.
We played football together.

It was brilliant!

Soon, everybody wanted
to play with me.

Now, I'm happy at school.
But I still **remember** how it
feels to be sad.

If I see someone who looks sad,

I try to **comfort** them.

I don't want anyone to feel as sad as I did.

Amy's story

I'm Amy. When I was three years old, my granny gave me a rabbit.

I called him Archie.

I played with Archie every day.

He looked funny when
he **twitched** his nose.

One day, Archie was ill.

We took him to the **vet**, but she couldn't make him better.

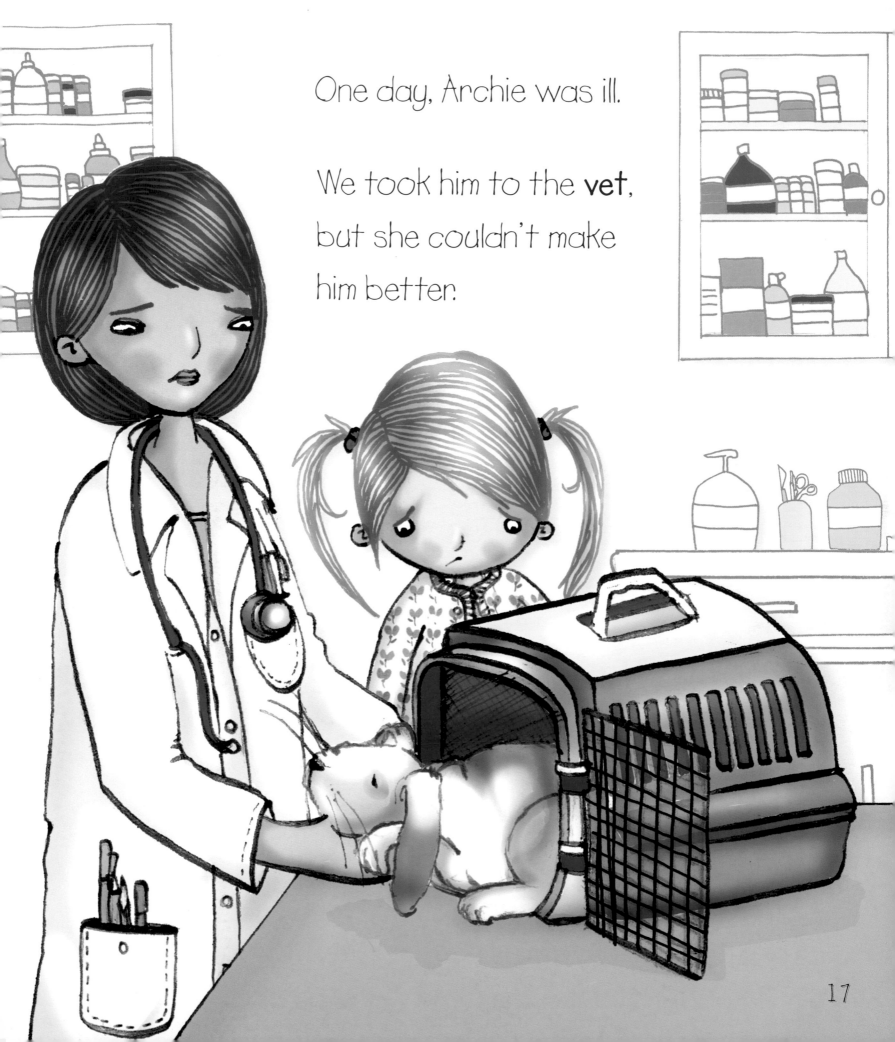

The next day, Archie died.

I felt very sad. I didn't want to eat any lunch.

In the afternoon, I looked at photos of Archie.

I remembered how he twitched his nose. I laughed and cried at the same time.

When I think about Archie now, I still feel sad.

But sometimes I feel happy, too. I have very
happy **memories** of him.

You can help

Do you know someone who is sad?

Perhaps you can talk to them, and help them feel better?

Glossary

comfort   when you comfort someone, you're kind to them and try to make them feel better

feelings   your feelings tell you how you are and what kind of mood you're in

forever   if something goes on forever, it never ends

lonely   if you are lonely, you feel unhappy because you're on your own

make friends   when you make friends, you get together with someone you like and who likes you, too

mean   if someone is mean to you, they are unkind and cruel

memories   if you have memories of someone, you still think about them and the things that they did

remember   when you remember something, you think about it again

tease   if people tease you, they say unkind things to you and laugh at you

twitch   if you twitch your nose, you move it from side to side

vet   a vet is someone who helps sick animals to get better. Vet is a short name for a veterinary surgeon.

Index

Notes for parents and teachers

- Look at the front cover of the book together. Talk about the picture. Can your children guess what the book is going to be about? Read the title together.

- Read the first line on page 4: 'People have lots of different feelings.' Help your children to make a list of different feelings.

- Ask your children to draw some simple faces showing different feelings. Then talk about their pictures. Which feelings make you feel good? Which don't feel so good?

- Read about what happened to Sam on his birthday (pages 4–5). Talk about Sam's feelings – first, when he was given his present, and then after he'd broken it.

- Read the question on page 5: 'When was the last time you felt sad?' Talk with your children about times when they've felt sad.

- Read about how it feels to be sad (pages 6–7). Ask your children how they feel when they're sad.

- Read page 8 together, and look at the picture of Sam. Ask your children how they think Sam feels now. Can your children remember when they were sad, but later they felt better?

- Read the first part of Omar's story together (pages 10–11). Ask your children how they think Omar feels. Talk about how it feels when people are mean to them. Can your children think of times when this has happened – either to them, or to someone they know?

- Ask your children to imagine how they could stop Omar feeling sad. Then read page 12 together, and talk about Zack. How did he make Omar feel better?

- Read the first part of Amy's story (pages 15–16). Ask your children to talk about their pet if they have one. Do they play with their pet every day like Amy?

- Read the next part of Amy's story together (pages 17–18). Ask your children how they think Amy feels now. Have they ever had a pet that died? How did they feel?

- Read the last part of Amy's story (pages 19–20). Talk about how it feels a little while after a pet has died. Do your children have happy memories of their pets?

- Your children may know a person who has died. If they want to talk about it, you could discuss how it feels when somebody you love dies. Talk about the happy memories that you have of a special person who has died.

- Look at page 21 together. Ask your children if they know anyone who is sad. What could they do to make their friend feel better?

- Role-play comforting a friend. Ask your children to take turns at being the one who is sad and the one who comforts them.